Love and Stones

Josephine Corcoran

Josephine Corcoran (born Southport, 1961) grew up in a loving family entirely dependent on state benefits for income and spent part of her childhood in foster care. Previous poetry collections are *What Are You After?* (Nine Arches Press, 2018) and *The Misplaced House* (tall-lighthouse, 2014). She also has two BBC R4 credits for an afternoon play and a short story, and a stage play was produced at the Chelsea Theatre in London. As a mature student, she studied at the universities of Bournemouth, Chichester, and East Anglia.

First Published in 2023
By Live Canon Poetry Ltd
www.livecanon.co.uk

978-1-909703-16-2

Cover image:

'Avebury Stones' by Sue Burns (Instagram @sketchsueburns)

Contents

Poem for a 1960s Welfare State Childhood

Each night I fell asleep in our council house
with no thought in my head that someone
would want to take away our home.
We moved rooms and beds depending on
who was ill, or home from college or work.

I took possession of the landing for play,
and the hallway, and windowsills painted gloss
to slide along, line-up my family of dolls.
I was given everything: school meals, milk,
uniform vouchers, bus fares, library books.

The man on my doorstep with a blue rosette
tells me I have it wrong. It's *luck* I've grown up
strong, secure, even when my world unravelled.
I'm misremembering how cared-for I felt.
And consider the cost!

I let him keep his leaflet
and tell my children how my sister
gave me her beautiful coat,
two sizes too big. *You'll grow,* she said
fastening me into love and my future.

Then, said I, Lord, How Long?

Beautiful, the man in my hallway
lacing up his second-hand shoes.
He is 18 years old, he is my son,
he is late, I have no money for him,
all my loose change
dropped in the church basket. *Holy Hell!*
They are using it to fly criminals around the world!

Waving goodbye is the man, shaved head
and beard, a time-lapse the hallway,
scuffed mornings. Boys and girls calling
to walk him to school, billowing
like fruits and flowers, disappearing –
reappearing like film stars to crowd
the hallway mirror, perfume the house.

Tripping over, stepping around
rucksacks, hats, gadgets, mud,
musical instruments, books,
sleeping bags, corner shop alcohol –
Did you hand in your essay?
Mum, the planet is dying –
Goodbye, goodbye, for 18 years, waving goodbye.

Hungry the baby, sucking his fists,
cold hospital February, scored plastic cot,
my skin already scabbing
and him three hours old,

as they stitched me, he latched on to my breast,
cuts on his face, bruises, mini prize fighter,
starched blanket, milk, the heat of him.

Next to the candles I sat, next to the Virgin Mary,
reading Isiah backwards
in my head, holding language
in my mouth to taste it longer.
desolate utterly be land the & man without houses the &
inhabitant without wasted be cities the until answered he
& long how Lord I said.

Then.
Give me a kiss then, Mum. I'm away.
Eighteen summers
shaken from trees, falling flowers, leaves
raining down, streaming
through park, town, along the street,
into my hallway, my childless house.

Stories Are What We Are

You tell me you drove up and back on this road
for over a year when the children were small.
You'd leave us sleeping, drive in the dark, turning
here, you'd see the sun rising. I don't recall
your hushed mornings. My world was a blur
of children and chores. We argued
in misspelt texts, scribbled notes.
Found apologies, kisses, in our pockets.

We stare at the landscape. Stonehenge
in the distance, grain in the fields, cattle grazing.
The road weaving through ancient places
of worshippers, mourners, settlers, hunters,
farmers, gatherers, and people
unsure of their role or their meaning.
I found a man here, you say. *One daybreak. Alone.*
In some kind of trouble.

Now you tell me the story.
A dense morning mist. You could've killed
the man. Swerved. Circled back. Saw the stag
dead at his feet, the car written off. The two
of you dragged the animal into shrubland,
the man still in shock, trembling, telling you it had leapt
out of the mist, on to the car – *as if he was being chased*
the man said.   I imagine him

glad of your help, holding on to your hands as you
said your goodbyes and retelling the story as you
have to me, as people have been telling such stories

for thousands of years. The kindness of strangers.
Chance meetings. Sleeping families.
Morning mists. Arguments in our heads. Love
in our pockets. Standing stones. Running deer.
Stories of death and stories of living.

To Love One Another

On Maundy Thursday, Anne whispered to me
Look at the state of him! He's not used to hard work!

By then, the choir were singing
something sorrowful,
altar servers clearing towels and bowls of water,
parishioners on the altar
readjusting socks and shoes.

Father Luke walked past us to the sacristy,
his face as red as beef, sweat like dripping candles.
We couldn't keep our faces straight.

That was the year a badger
was digging up my garden.
Even when I shifted huge stones
from the rockery to keep him out
he found a way of shoving them aside,
clawed a tunnel under my fence.

I thought of all the feet she and I
had washed throughout our lives.
I thought of women
in the church, our work
of washing feet. Not only feet – bodies
that we'd hoisted, cleaned,
dressed, comforted many times.

There never seems a chance for us
to talk. We've met each week for years,
sitting, kneeling, standing
side by side, whispering hello, goodbye,
holding hands for the sign of peace.

At the Easter Vigil, when it came to the stone –
large and rolled away – she whispered to me
that it was like my badger and that set us off again

our shoulders going hell for leather
while all the bells were jingling.

To Bring Me Luck

I stop the bridal carriage
at an old people's home, choose
the wisest, oldest woman, pretend
that she's my mother, hold her
to me like a new shawl.

Lent an abundance
of promises and warnings
I borrow it all
though my mother discards most things
but knowledge and power

and climbs down from my shoulders
to buy two pairs
of good blue running shoes.
We lace each other up. Our pockets
jangling with silver sixpences.

True Crime

Home alone, dinner on my knees
I binge on all eight episodes
not sleeping until the early hours
when the two detectives
lock away a serial rapist
their colleagues had overlooked.

Next day, channel surfing,
I'm spoilt for choice. Serial killers,
rapists, violent burglary, assault,
battery, kidnap, coercion, GBH,
strangulation, mutilation –
I step over each dead woman
as I climb the stairs to bed.

Visiting Woodhenge
and The Church of St Mary and St Melor, Amesbury

It is the story of a woman
whose understanding travels dreamlike
between two places. One scorching day

she adds her fingerprints
to a stone-and-timber neolithic circle,
to an early church.

Time, a dandelion clock.
Knowing, unknowing, she steps
on footprints, belongings, bones –

returning and returning to a mound of flint,
a small inhumation. Flowers and grasses
shaped like circles. Little offerings.

Mary's robes, blue as cloudlessness,
upright baby in her arms. Cool stone walls
forgive the heatwave. Rows of shining candles.

She has read poems. Heard mother
cows outside a slaughterhouse. Cried
in cinemas at scenes of small unslept-in beds.

In newspapers, history books, read
of disappearances, violence, children
owned, bartered, sacrificed,

stored all this, her heart an aching place,
plot of ancient pain
where coins are thrown for luck & children

make daisy chains, singing wishes
while parents hold up their phones like torches.
No holy water in the font, but gypsophila.

She dips her hand in baby's breath,
also known as maiden's breath,
closes her eyes in sunlight, as if she is half-waking.

Parenting Book

I wrote it down when you woke me at 3am
to tell me you didn't like ham anymore.
Only jam. And cheese. How the shower cubicle
was where a murderer would lurk.

I kept a notebook for years. The sore throat
bad as three arrows sticking into it.
Rosanna in the Highest
who went to church. It didn't last.

You learned eventually
to not ask visitors
Did you have a good Christmas?
when they came to our house in June,

stopped shouting comments
on the bus
about *disgusting* perfume.
How your teacher *looked* beautiful

but was horrible inside.
Before I knew it, you were buying
condoms on the internet,
marching for Human Rights

and I'd fall asleep
wondering
who's dancing in a club,
who's buying chips from a van

and I'd wake up
to the smell of toast burning,
a voice calling
I've fixed it! Everything's fine!

While Shepherds Watch is playing on the radio,
a tea towel headdress lies in a drawer.
The final page, you scribbled me a note.
Some kind of map. Half a silver star.

Child's Play

That game we played
        you, skipping down the street
        your brother in his buggy
so many sirens screaming past.

You always asked
What do you think happened?
and loved the convoluted stories
made up your own

        a break-in at a chocolate factory
        one enormous tree, one tiny kitten
until you started school
retired from skipping.

In playground huddles
you whispered
in the ears of friends
looked at me accusingly

as if you'd read
the headlines, seen
the crying families, learned
the children's names.

In Lockdowns, People Notice More Birdsong

My chicks fly home
as I am dismantling the empty nest.
Panic!
How will I feed them?
Food's in short supply.

I flap down the road
in time to the thuds
of footballs in yards,
Every other house shaking
with DIY.

The council tweets
No tree-netting today.
No hedgerow-slashing.
The pesticide-sprayer
is staying inside.

I glide over streets
singing
caterpillars, spiders,
beetles and grubs.
My children sing their reply.

Once Upon a Lockdown, 2020

Rosebud
Once upon a tightly folded rosebud a letter from the Prime Minister arrives. It is Friday. Or maybe Monday. There are bluebells in the garden. I wash out jars: jam, pickle, marmalade. Bring buttercups inside. The supermarket emails about queues. My shelves are flower-filled. In my Instagram window, I listen to the news. Perhaps it's Tuesday.

Unfolding
Once upon a rose unfolding in a living room, we unfold a static bike and cycle, cycle, cycle. On Thursdays we bang a saucepan with a spoon. We cycle, cycle, cycle, walk in local streets. In windows, children hold up rainbows.

Pink and Mauve
It is April, it is May. Every day feels like Sunday in the Seventies, once upon full blooming, pink and mauve. Our children went to uni, imagining themselves grown. They are sleeping, sleeping, sleeping in childhood beds. Their heads lie next to fairy tales. Roses smell of strawberry jam. There are scratches on our skin.

We are stranded online when daybreak arrives.
Once upon not dreaming about roses, we move through rooms like sunlight making shapes on walls, keeping different hours. We meet at midnight, at 4am, in the kitchen, on the stairs, exchanging notes about our dreams: driving to a roadblock, the pubs are open, love is in our arms. A professor rifles through a lunchbox selecting cakes. A dream about thermometers, a dream about escape. There is anger in our dreams. I appear in dreams, being ineffectual.

Each Petal Falling

Once upon each falling petal, many falling petals, forty thousand, forty-one thousand, fifty-two thousand, sixty thousand, and counting, counting, counting. It is June.

Compost

Their heads are drooping now, like loved ones who sat for long days inside locked-up television rooms. Petals of discoloured tissues in a time of weeping. Each day another slumped and silent silhouette. We carry them to compost, remembering their radiance, refusing to forget.

In Lockdown, Solitude Becomes a Flying Lover
(after a postcard of 'Over the Town' by Marc Chagall)

Children leave for their student lives,
husband catches an early train. In bed,
I hear the front door snap, steam rising
from an affectionate cup of tea, and you
move in, the one who loves me most.

I sleep as sunlight kisses walls, silent
luggage trundling by, your gentle tread.
And so, it goes. Long afternoons. Bread
gingerly becoming toast. Ink
flowering on my fingers as I write.

You choose empty rooms, listening
to the drifting talk of pipes. Above a fireplace,
the postcard leans. Each house receives
its morning dust and lovers stream
through weightless time. Then, a letter

from the Prime Minister, his daily briefings.
Here are the children returning to a childhood
they no longer want. Here comes my husband.
Laptops and wires. Each room bristling
with its weather. Snow of electronic noise.

Furniture uncloseable
as a swollen door. On the floor,
strange springtime of belongings.
The postcard slips
behind a long-forgotten clock.

I cannot stop myself
lifting from the ground. You join me
like an answered call, turn your head –
I reach beyond the town.
We hold each other. To look down
would be to fall.

A Baby Speaks on his Birthday
in an Autumn Garden, 2020

It's the equinox, time for a cake and candle –
your first – although we're not allowed
to be with you. Instead, we hold you
in our kitchens like a lantern, your face
inside our phones, small bringer of light.

For half your life, your world
has been your Mum and Dad,
house, garden, local street. You know
nothing, yet, of your big extended family.

Look at the colours, Sweetheart!
Your Mum films you scrambling into autumn,
leaves sparking orange, parched as kindle,
scratch and crackle through your knees and hands.

None of us understand this virus, shaken loose
from burning forests. Denial
breathes inside our masks
and you make gentle sounds for each twig, branch,
root and leaf you honour with your deep attention.

What a garden! someone says, in lieu of counting
the daily deaths. Fizzing with energy
you raise both arms, spilling autumn towards
aunties, uncles, cousins - words you've never heard

our voices calling through the universe
of flaming creepers, burnt gold berries, scorched
tangle of vines ablaze on fences, roses faded
as if kissed with soot.
We hear you telling us to *Look!*

Circles and Wildflowers

circle of bluebells
circus of columbine
halo of daisies
hoop of ransoms

arena of musk mallow
ring of teasels
orbit of cowslips
spiral of cuckoo flowers

loop of cow parsley
band of thrift
wreath of dog rose briars
revolution of field scabious

clock of common yarrow
sphere of ragged robin

circle & circus & loop & spiral
of field poppies, meadow cranes,
corncrackle, cornflowers

sun of buttercups
moon of harebells

Sheep at Avebury Stones

not us   not grass   not human are these
          not giving way   not tumbling   here
                                        making long dark
here   lit by sun   humans appear
disappear   we move   between
          these   not human   not grass   not us
          we move   stand next to   push against

sun   then not sun
appears disappears   now moon
          now not moon   now sun

          we release steaming liquid   we gift
grass-full droppings   we eat we
          release we gift we eat we release
               we gift move stand next to push
and there are humans   humanshumans
humans   moving touching talking
to
               not us
                    not human   not
grass
                              our wool caught
                              here

sun rises   falls between   sun rises

               falls

notes on a patio that was sprayed with weedkiller

one black ant on april roads.
each paving slab a place of no
verges, ditches, hedgerows, boughs.
one thread of grass.

one bright forager, sent out for news.
curious in empty squares.
was it here? is this where? will I find?
one dandelion, smaller than before.

one strand of human hair. broken
spider's web. litter of fragmental leaves.
each site unswept. one incinerated
wood louse. one snail shell, hollow

as an abandoned bus. sprinkling
of partial heads & wings. two ants
rock forward, back, lifting morsels
of a life. may brings slow blooming.

a border shrub, thin white buds.
planet of lice & beetles under
a discarded plate. a pigeon
dips its beak in shallow rain.

late june, sparse roses. one quiet bee
hesitates. this flower? this? turns, tips
into muffled perfume. frail glow of
distant strawberry. one ant continues

stealing through rain, wind, sunshine
to nearly august now. pale
rose petals blow through
a smooth concrete landscape.

by the outside tap, one lovely
avenue of tiny clover, green & plum.
one small ant trembles, trembles.
such heavy cargo it carries home.

Last Chance, Strawberries

We wave goodbye to the children
and drive away, past honey-coloured farmland

towards Salisbury Plain. It's late July,
no rain for months, and everything blue

seems risen to the sky, gold
shining in our mirrors as our car rolls by

fields of barley, wheat, corn. Twenty-five years
and our first time alone here. Signs blink at us

in the tawny light. *Cherries! Strawberries For Sale!*
little boxes stacked on tables to the side,

a pictogram of a leaping deer, cows grazing
on the bumps and mounds of longbarrows.

Larkhill, Stonehenge, Historic Amesbury.
You tell me this was school trip territory

and I see you scowling in a photo
at your Mum's house, childhood

mysterious as the landscape.
The traffic slows and I stare

at tourists standing still, staring
at ancient stones. You share stories

you've kept for years: burial chambers,
long- bowl- oval- bell-shaped barrows,

stone circles, crop circles, henges. *Last Chance
Strawberries* reads a sign on a scrap of cardboard.

Let's not leave here without tasting
a handful of something wild and sweet.

sunflowers exist, sunflowers exist
after Inger Christensen translated by Susanna Nied

sunflowers exist, sunflowers exist;

in summer, sunflowers exist
for the first time in my garden;

last spring, neighbours gave me seedlings & seeds,
said my garden would sing with sweetpeas, strawberries,
sunflowers & birdsong; birdsong exists, songbirds exist

singing, singing; from overhanging trees
squirrels break in to steal sunflowers;
there's stealing & crime scenes while songbirds are singing
& strawberries are falling & sweetpeas are spiralling;
crime scenes exist while sunflowers are shining;

streets of sameness exist, the ground dusty with sickness;
stones exist where there used to be gardens; stony
patches, sterile as crime scenes, where there used to be
spiders & slugs in the gardens & shade from trees filled
with songbirds, like nightingale, blackbird, woodlark, mistle
thrush, skylark, song thrush, robin, also sparrow & starling
now nestless; how can I feel smug holding my sunflowers
when starlings are nestless; but sweet-scented meadows

exist; I have grown my grass long, counted poppies,
buttercups, dandelions, daisies, forget-me-nots, celandines,
clover; but sulphur dioxide exists; hydrocarbons, nitrogen
oxides, the burning of fossil fuels, the smelting of minerals
but my sunflowers exist shining light in my garden, though
sickness is hovering where there used to be hoverflies,
dragonflies, bees, wasps, bats & moths, where there used
to be caterpillars, beetles, spiders & ants & fat starlings
now nestless; but sweetpeas are spiralling, strawberries are
falling but satellites in orbit carrying laser weapons exist;
shooting stars and shooting both exist & soldiers exist
at scenes of a crime, scenes of a war crime, soldiers who
kissed their lovers, last summer in fields of sunflowers;

sunflowers, their sequence, their pattern, now ruptured
in seasons, disrupted; springtime, disrupted, broken
promises of birdsong, like kisses, now soldiers with guns;
six million shares of a film on a smartphone,
the old woman saying "put these seeds in your pockets
so that sunflowers will grow; when you all lie down here,
sunflowers will grow";
soldiers holding the thought of a sunflower.

Seen While Walking
eight floral nightdresses on a washing line

In this house, someone moves
in each pink gloss-painted window
sipping tea, knees tucked under roses
and geraniums. Passers-by
raise their phones but later find
their own reflections, heads
full-blown, petals spilling
forwards, waving.

Acknowledgements

'Poem for a 1960s Welfare State Childhood' (*The Morning Star*); 'Then, Said I, Lord How Long?' (*Poetry Wales*); 'To Bring Me Luck' (Commended in the Poetry Society's 2018 Stanza Competition, judged by Penelope Shuttle); 'True Crime' and 'To Love One Another' (*The North*); 'Parenting Book' (*Ink, Sweat and Tears*); 'Once upon a Lockdown, 2020' (*The Great Margin, Bath Spa University*); 'notes made on a patio that was sprayed with weedkiller' (Highly Commended, *Teignmouth Poetry Competition, 2022,* judged by Katrina Naomi); 'A Baby Speaks on His Birthday in an Autumn Garden, 2020' (Shortlisted *Live Canon International Poetry Competition, 2020,* judged by Jennifer Wong); 'Visiting Woodhenge and the Church of St Mary and St Melor, Amesbury' (Shortlisted *Live Canon International Poetry Competition, 2022,* judged by Rebecca Goss); 'Sheep at Avebury' (Longlisted, *Rialto Nature and Place Competition, 2020,* judged by Pascale Petit); 'In Lockdowns, People Notice More Birdsong' (*Ledbury Poetry Festival website*); 'Seen While Walking: eight floral nightdresses on a washing line' (*Under the Radar*). 'In Lockdown, Solitude Becomes a Flying Lover' and 'sunflowers exist, sunflowers exist' (*UEA New Writing*)

I am grateful to Bloor Homes/Ginkgo Projects for a Local Artist's Bursary which supported the writing of some of these poems.

Thank you to all at Live Canon, especially Helen Eastman.

Love and thanks to my siblings and cousins and their families, and especially to Andrew, Kitty and Johnny.

LIVE CANON